KILLERS
OF
CHILDREN

(A Psychoanalytic Look at Sex Education)

©Melvin Anchell, M.D., A.S.P.P.
American Life League
188 Onville Rd.
Stafford, VA 22554
(703) 659-4171

BOOKS BY MELVIN ANCHELL, M.D.

How I Lost 36,000 Pounds

Understanding Your Sexual Needs

Sex and Sanity

A Second Look at Sex Education

Sex and Insanity

DEDICATED TO:

Christine deVollmer

Whose efforts to maintain decency in Western culture knows no boundries.

FOR

decent people -- loving people in our Nation, who, in an environment gone mad with unbridled physical sex, exemplify the life sustaining nature of human sexuality.

By example they teach their children the wonder of sexually fulfilled man/woman monogamous love --- the meaning of life itself.

Table of Contents

ii

A. THE FACTS OF HUMAN SEXUALITY

Public school sex education programs have been established in schools throughout the United States for over two decades.

Before discussing these programs and the harm they cause students and society, three basic psychoanalytical facts concerning human sexuality should be mentioned. These three truths are inherent and they apply to all people throughout the world.

The first established truth is that in humans "sex is an intimate affair" .... two people in love seek total privacy during their sexual intimacies.

Intrusions of others into their physical sexual life, normally arouse intense feelings of shame and jealousy in both men and women.

Jealousy is one of those affective states, like grief, that may be described as normal. If anyone appears to be without it, the inference is justified that it has undergone severe repression and consequently plays all the greater part in his unconscious mental life.

.... normal jealousy is compounded of grief, the pain caused by the thought of losing the loved object and .... of feelings of enmity against the successful rival and .... of some self criticism which tries to hold the person himself accountable for his loss.

Sensuality and the Psychology of Love
by Sigmund Freud

The more two people are in love, the more they suffice for each other. It is only when love is lacking that people are able to share physical sex with a series of partners or in groups. When this takes place, a regression occurs to a primitive state in which love plays no part in the sex act.

To repeat, the first fact is, that intimate love is an inborn characteristic of human sexuality. Its need to be limited to two people only is prescribed by the very nature of the sex act itself.

Today's public school sex programs disregard this initial fact concerning human sexuality.

The second psychoanalytic fact is that in humans, the sexual instinct is composed of two currents -- an affectionate current and a physical current. The affectionate component is as important — if not more so — than the physical component.

For human sexuality to be complete, there must be a confluence, a coming together, of the affectionate and physical components of sex. When affectionate needs are weakened and physical sex is all that remains, "sex becomes meaningless and life becomes empty."

Throughout public school sex classrooms, physical aspects of sex are emphasized while affectionate needs are damned by faint praise.

To believe that psychoanalysis seeks a cure for neurotic disorders by giving a free rein to sexuality is a serious misunderstanding which can only be justified by ignorance.

Psychoanalysis,
by Sigmund Freud

The third basic fact is that in humans, unlike any other creature, three phases of sexual development occur before adult sexual maturity is reached.

The first phase begins at birth and lasts through the 5th year of life.

The second phase of human sexual development occurs between the ages of 6-12, and

The third stage of sexual development starts around the age of 13 and continues into early adulthood.

Vann Spruniell, M.D. (Psychoanalyst, Associate Professor of Psychiatry, Tulane University), in an article, "Don't Force Grown-up Sex Education on Children," *Medical Economics Magazine*, December 6, 1971:

Dr. Warren J. Gadpaille [American Association of Sex Educators and Counselors and Consultant on Family Living Programs]...would provide, from kindergarten through high school, information about anatomy, "dirty" words, procreation, sexual attitudes and sexual practices. All this would be derived from instruction, small-animal demonstrations and a series of "frank discussions."

What of respected scientific opinion that sex education might be "too much, too soon?"

Today's public school sex education -- which, incidentally, Planned Parenthood now euphemistically refers to as "Family Life Programs" -- is not in accord with natural sexual growth processes occurring in the three phases of human sexual development, thereby making it virtually impossible for sexually educated students to grow into sexually mature adults.

To understand "why and how" today's Planned Parenthood sponsored sex programs cause such irreparable harm to students, let's briefly look at the three phases of human sexual growth and, at the same time, also look at the sex teaching given to students during each of the three developmental phases.

FIRST PHASE

B. HUMAN SEXUAL DEVELOPMENT

PHASE I

The first phase of human sexual development, as previously mentioned, begins at birth and lasts through the 5th year of life. (It should be noted that the 1st phase itself is divided into three stages.)

The initial sensual pleasure in life is derived from the sucking that is associated with the infant's need for nourishment. From the very beginning it can be seen that *normal* sensual pleasure is associated with life sustaining needs.

The sucking — or oral stage — usually comes to an end around the 2nd year of life at which time the child's main sensual pleasure is then attained from "aggressive-anal" impulses.

Sensual aggressiveness consists of the desire to master another by force rather than by wooing. It may seem strange that the predominant sensual urge in a small 2 year old child is derived from aggressiveness, but such pleasure may not seem so surprising if one realizes that cruelty is a primitive vestige that remains a part of the sexual instinct.

The aggressive second stage passes into the third childhood sexual stage at about the age of 3 and continues through the 5th year of life.

During the ages of 3-5, the child's primary sensual pleasure is derived from the desire "to see and show nudity." Therefore, this stage is exhibitionistic and voyeuristic in nature. It can be readily seen, for example, in the innocent but unmistakable sensual excitment that some three-to-five year old children exhibit when gleefully running about the room nude after a bath.

Normally the first phase of early childhood sexual growth consisting of oral, aggressive and exhibitionistic-voyeuristic impulses is passed through smoothly and usually give only fleeting glimpses of its development.

"There is only one factor in childhood which has such central importance that its impairment calls for immediate action: that is the child's ability to develop, not to remain fixed to any (sexual) stage of development.

The seriousness of a childhood neurosis should be assessed not according to the damage which it does to the child but according to the degree in which it prevents the child from further (sexual) development."

The Psychoanalytical Treatment of Children

by Anna Freud

Children *must not* be made to linger in these beginning stages of sexual growth.

If misguided adults, sex educators or child molestors cause the child to linger in oral, aggressive or exhibitionistic-voyeuristic infantile sensual activities, an arrest, that is, a fixation in these early stages may occur and further forward sexual growth may cease. This is exactly what may result from the sex programs given to 3-5 year old kindergarten students.

Twenty-five years ago, I and many other child analysts might have enthusiastically endorsed school sex education...because we believed at that time that emphasis on sexual knowledge could do no harm, only good. We have since learned that it is harmful to force sexual preoccupation on children ....forcing of sexual preoccupation on the elementary school child is very likely to result in sexual difficulties in adulthood, and it can lead to disturbed behavior in childhood.

Rhoda L. Lorand, Ph.D.
(Psychologist, New York City)

".... sensual impulses operate normally in the youngest children without any need for outside stimulation."

*Freud's Letters 70 and 71
to W. Fliess*

Kindergarten sex instructions consist of openly displaying nudity, of demonstrating male and female genital anatomy, and of showing how humans as well as some animals mate.

The 3-5 year old has absolutely no need for such sex interferences. The instructions have no beneficial effect and can only serve to disrupt the child's further forward sexual growth by causing a fixation in early childhood sensual stages.

Sexual interferences damages the child's forward movement of sexual development. Sex organization flows backwards (regression) and attaches itself once more to earlier sensual wishes (fixation point). The ego of the child finds itself confronted with primitive desires (oral, aggressive, anal).

From the developmental point of view, what counts is that sexual development is arrested in its course. Instead of moving on towards adult levels, it has been forced backwards, and important gains have thereby been undone. Qualities and achievements which depend directly on the stage of sexual growth are lost.

The child who regresses to an oral level, for instance, reverts to the emotional attitudes associated with it: it becomes more insatiable, impatient, "like a baby." Regression from the exhibitionistic-voyeuristic stage to the aggressive-anal stage destroys the hardly acquired attitudes of generosity, manliness and protectiveness and substitutes for them the domineering possessiveness which belongs to the earlier stage.

The Psychoanalytical Treatment of Children

by Anna Freud

For example, repeated demonstrations of nudity and genital anatomy given in kindergarten sex classes cause undue intensification of and lingering in exhibitionism and voyeurism.

As a result, forward sexual growth may cease and "seeing and showing" becomes the main sexual aim from then on. In such cases, the eye replaces the genital organ as the primary sexual site in later life.

Every environmental influence that hinders (sexual growth) will evidently lend support to the tendency to linger over the preparatory activities and turn them into new sexual aims that can take the place of the normal one.

Three Essays on the Theory of Sexuality

by Sigmund Freud

".... there is no period at which the capacity for receiving and reproducing impressions is greater than precisely the years of childhood."

Sigmund Freud

Indeed, over the years, the widespread interferences by sex educators in the sexual development of the 3-5 year old can be seen in the ever increasing exhibitionism and voyeurism that has become part of our everyday culture. Pornographic books and magazines are available at practically every newsstand and there are few, if any, movies that fail to show nudity and, at least, one intimate bedroom scene.

$100's of millions of dollars are spent each year by today's young people just for pornographically-oriented videotapes and records alone. So it can be seen that what is learned in childhood leaves impressions that remain throughout life.

"Psychoanalysis shows an impression of this kind in early childhood contributes a great deal towards a predisposition to a subsequent sadism."

Sigmund Freud

The kindergarten sex instructions given to 3-5 year olds regarding mating causes still further problems. Psychoanalysis has shown that when a child is permitted to watch people mate (whether supervised by a sex teacher or not) the sex act is invariable regarded as a sadistic subjugation -- i.e., an abuse -- of the female.

The cruelty feelings in children subjected to such demonstrations of "coitus in the classroom" may be strengthened, and an excessive amount of sadism and masochism may come to play a major role in their adult sex life.

Another problem that may result from kindergarten sex education is that during the ages of 3-5 there are brief intervals in which the child has inclinations to fondle its genitals. If, through the teachings of sex instructors or a child molestor, a child is encouraged to linger in such genital sex play and learns to obtain heightened satisfaction from the genital organ, the child is then usually obliged to repeat this satisfaction again and again. Through the instinct of repetition, incessant masturbation may continue right through childhood, into adolescence and adulthood. This would constitute the first major deviation in normal, civilized sexual development.

Consider for just one moment one example of what could happen as a result of such an aberration --- a girl child, for example, led to engage in repeated clitoral sex play by a child molestor or kindergarten sex instructions may grow up to become a nymphomaniac.

The life of a nymphomaniac is a shambles, for her, the sex act is merely a compulsive affectionateless urge to repeat her early fixation in clitoral sex play. Any man who will participate with her is considered a suitable partner. Her appetite for sex is like the alcoholic's for liquor -- she can never get enough, she is never satisfied and she gets no pleasure from it. There is no worldly chance that she will ever be capable of making a mature, life sustaining sexual adjustment irrespective of whether or not she gets married, has children or whatever.

"The sexual theories of children show more understanding of sexual processes than one would have given them credit for. Children also perceive the alterations that take place in their mother owning to pregnancy and are able to interpret them correctly.

The sexual researches of these early years of childhood are always carried out in solitude. They constitute a first step towards taking an independent attitude in the world."

Sigmund Freud

A brief review, then, of the harm done by kindergarten sex teachings given during the first phase of human sexual development is:

One: (1) These instructions may cause an arrest in forward sexual growth and produce a lifelong fixation in childhood exhibitionistic-voyeuristic sensual pleasures which become the primary sexual aim making a mature sexual adjustment in later life highly improbable.

Two: (2) Demonstrations of mating given the 3-5 year old strengthen "aggressive-cruelty feelings" which may lead to sadistic-masochistic dispositions when these children grow up.

Three: (3) Kindergarten sex teachings encourage an undue lingering in genital sex play which may cause continuous masturbation throughout childhood, adolescence and adulthood. Such masturbatory practices weaken character and preclude the development of mature adult sexuality.

Before concluding these brief comments on the first phase of sexual development and of the harm done by kindergarten sex programs, one important additional finding should be mentioned.

In the cases of many homosexuals, even 100% ones, it is possible to show that very early in their lives a sexual impression occured which left a permanent after-effect in the shape of a tendency to homosexuality.

In the case of many others, it is possib'e to point to environmental influences in their lives which have led sooner or later to a fixation of their homosexuality.

Homosexuality can be removed by hypnotic suggestion, which would be astonishing in an inborn characteristic.

....if the cases of allegedly inborn homosexuality were more closely examined, some experience of their early childhood would probably come to light which had a determining effect upon the direction taken by their sexuality. The experience would simply have passed out of the subject's conscious recollection, but could be recalled to his memory under appropriate influence.

*Three Essays on the Theory
of Sexuality*

by Sigmund Freud

Contrary to the teachings promulgated by sex educators that perversions, such as homosexuality, are due to "glandular or inherited conditions," over 100 years of psychoanalytic observations in real clinical settings have unequivocally shown that adult perverts are primarily a product of premature sexual experiences or seductions in early childhood.

This is true whether the seduction is due to actual attacks by a child molestor, or whether the seduction is due to overexposures to sexual activities in sex classrooms or in the pornographic media.

SECOND PHASE

C. HUMAN SEXUAL DEVELOPMENT

PHASE II

We now come to the second phase of human sexual development which occurs between the ages of 6-12.

As before, let us briefly look at the second phase of human sexual development and at the same time consider the effects of today's public school sex programs on 6-12 year old children.

Vann Spruniell, M.D. (Psychoanalyst):

They [psychiatrists] constantly observe latency — the real "McCoy", not just a deceptive appearance of it...during latency, the child develops an inner control system...

During latency, adult communication with him about adult sex is an intrusion into an important and necessary privacy.

The second sexual phase is referred to throughout the world as the "latency period." It is a period in which nature causes direct sexual energies in the 6-12 year old child to become dormant. There is nothing hypothetical about the latency period. It has been shown to exist throughout the world --- in primitive as well as civilized people.

William McGrath, M.D. (Psychiatrist)

There is a phase of personality development called the latency period, during which the healthy child is not interested in sex. This interval from about the age of five until adolescence serves a very important biological purpose. It affords a child an opportunity to develop his own resources, his beginning physical and mental strength.

Premature interest in sex is unnatural and will arrest or distort the development of the personality. Sex education should not be foisted on children;........

Though direct sexual energies become quiescent during latency, these energies do not disappear but are redirected by the 6-12 year old mind and are used to serve other purposes. For example, some redirected sexual energy is used for acquiring knowledge. This is why the 6-12 year old child is most educable.

"In so far as educators pay any attention to childhood sexuality .... they behave as though they knew that sexual activity makes a child ineducable."

Sigmund Freud

Prior to the establishment of today's public school sex teachings, teachers seemed to realize that involving the 6-12 year old child in sexual matters made the child ineducable; and they made every effort to avoid arousing the child sexually.

Sociologists Peter R. Uhlenberg and David Eggebeen of the University of North Carolina focus on the changes in the welfare of white teenagers from 1960 to 1980, as indicated by statistics measuring their educational performance, moral character, and physical health.

The facts are not very reassuring. In the 20-year interval, the Scholastic Aptitude Test scores of college-bound high school seniors declined steeply, and the high-school dropout rate increased. At the same time, delinquency rates, drug use, and childbirth and abortion rates for unmarried teenage women all rose sharply.

Whatever the reasons for these disturbing trends, economic factors do not appear to be primary ones. The authors point out that the incidence of poverty among white youths 16 and 17 years old, for example, declined by 60% from 1960 to 1980. In the same period, real per-pupil expenditures in U.S. public schools doubled, a change reflected in both a drop in class size and an increase in the percentage of teachers with graduate degrees. Federal social programs aimed at the young also proliferated.

In short, write Uhlenberg and Eggebeen, "spending more money to improve the environments of children has not brought about an improvement in their well-being."

from,

Economic Diary

Repeated scholastic tests done on today's sexually educated 6-12 year old children, indeed, show that these students have accomplished less scholastically than pre-sex education students.

"The absence of the barrier of compassion brings with it the danger that the connection between cruelty and the sexual instincts may prove unbreakable."

Sigmund Freud

The educability of children is not all that is at stake when latency is disturbed by classroom sex interferences.

For example, during latency, some redirected sexual energy is used for the development of compassion. Compassion is essential for the control of cruelty impulses in the human. Compassion is one of the elements that truly separates man from all other creatures.

If compassion fails to develop during latency due to direct sexual energies being kept stirred up by school sex programs, it is most unlikely to develop at any other time in life.

During the latency period, the child's interest in sexual matters largely subsides....

Within the framework of the family, the child is now freed from the dross of sexuality. Tenderness takes the place of erotic needs, activity that of infantile aggression, etc.

from *"Prepuberty"*

by Psychiatrist Helene Deutsch
Boston Psychoanalytic
Institute

In addition to these things already mentioned, latency makes invaluable contributions to personal and cultural achievements.

Finally, and most important, latency is also responsible for strengthening inborn mental barriers that control base sexual and aggressive instincts.

These mental barriers "or restraints," consist of feelings of shame, disgust, moral ideas, aesthetics, pain, horror, etc.

These barriers are inborn and are essential for controlling raw sexual and aggressive instincts.

Our civilization is founded on the suppression of instincts. Each individual has contributed some renunciation....

Over and above the struggle for existence, it is chiefly family feeling...., which has induced the individuals to make this renunciation. This renunciation.... is sanctioned by religion.

Sexuality and the Psychology of Love

by Sigmund Freud

Though inborn, to be effective in later life these mental barriers must be strengthened during the years of 6-12 by family, school and religion.

Among the instincts, the sexual instincts are conspicuous for their strength and savagery. Woe, if they should be set loose!

from *Character and Culture*

by Sigmund Freud

Instead of strengthening these controls, however, school sex courses use every educational technique known to break down these natural forces.

Removing mental controls over base sexuality is completely contrary to and destructive to family life and normal civilized sexuality.

Not infrequently, sex educators applaud the unrestrained, brazen attitudes of their sexually instructed 6-12 year old students, and proclaim that such personality traits are evidence of increased self- confidence.

However, the personality traits that the educators applaud are, frequently, the early characteristics of an uncaring psychopath --that is, an individual who has no concern for anyone but himself or others in so far as they can serve some purpose for him.

".…stirring-up of infantile sexuality is ultimately due to environmental interference."

Sigmund Freud

The psychopathy in today's sexually educated 6-12 year old children has reached alarming proportions. Preteen murders, pregnancies, prostitution, criminality and venereal diseases are no longer uncommon.

This increase in crimes, violence, and sex over the past 20 years is even more shocking when one considers that the six to twelve year old child, who has not been sexually disturbed, is normally a most responsible individual and one least likely to be involved in sociopathic behavior.

"Experience further showed that external influences are capable of provoking interruptions of the latency period or even its cessation."

Sigmund Freud

To sum-up, then: some adverse effects of the sex education courses given to 6-12 year old children are:

One: (1) Sex teachings make the 6-12 year old student less educable:

Two: (2) The courses can block the development of compassionate feelings:

Three: (3) The sex indoctrinations weaken mental barriers controlling base sexuality, thereby making the child vulnerable to perversions, and:

Four: (4) The teachings hamper social, cultural and personal achievements.

THIRD PHASE

D. HUMAN SEXUAL DEVELOPMENT

PHASE III

We now come to the third phase of human sexual development and to the sex courses given to adolescent students.

The third phase begins in puberty, around the age of thirteen, and continues throughout adolescence into early adulthood.

In this final phase of sexual development, latency comes to an end and direct sexual feelings are, once again, reawakened. In the case of 13 year old boys, the reawakened sexual energies are straight-forward and are centered in the genitalia. The reawakened erotic feelings of pubescent girls follows a *much* different course.

Because a girl's genital structures are (1) biologically unready and (2) remain anesthetic to sexual intercourse until much later in life, and (3) because her feminine psychology is not completed until late adolescence, *nature has provided the young female with a "natural aversion" to sexual intercourse.*

Though nature has provided the teenage girl with a natural aversion to engaging in the sex act, her sensual feelings may be as intense as the boy's. Her desires, however, are not for genital intercourse; but, instead, involve sexual fantasies and dreams, kisses and caresses, the wish to love and to be loved, tender words of love, and sometimes thoughts of having a child. Her erotic feelings, however, are not inseparably entwined with the sex act such as they are in the male.

Love fantasies in adolescent girls are natural, beneficial means for expressing their sexual needs.

Such fantasies are absolutely essential for the development of the feminine personality.

Many acts of gangsterism, prostitution or criminality in young girls are the consequence of a violent interruption of early puberty with its harmless girl-girl relationships by heterosexual acts for which they are not yet really ready ....

Premature heterosexual experiences produce disturbances in the development of a girl's whole personality.

from *The Psychology of Women*
by Helene Deutsch, M.D.

Today's sexually educated teenage female, who fails to abide by her natural feminine inhibitions and is led by sex teachings to prematurely engage in sex, reacts with feelings of (1) disappointment, (2) coldness and (3) emptiness. Due to engaging in intercourse prematurely, (1) her feminine psychology fails to develop, (2) her feminine emotions become dry and sterile and (3) a life-long conflict develops between herself and her inner femininity and motherhood feelings.

The dichotomy between the adolescent boy's readiness for sex and the girl's natural sexual inhibition serves a vital purpose. Nature always has a reason for what it does.

The girl's reluctance to the sex act serves to strengthen the affectionate and spiritual nature of sex. Adolescent female chastity is essential for development of affectionate relationships and for the spiritualization of sex.

Through sexual spiritualization, adolescents learn to regard sex and the sex partner with utmost importance.

Through sexual spiritualization, youths learn to feel esteem for members of the opposite sex. In the male, this esteem is especially felt for girls who are chaste --- and is usually lacking for girls who are easily had.

When affectionate needs are not met during sexual intercourse and physical sex is all that remains, frustrations result which frequently lead to serious depressions. For relief from these mental depressions, many of today's sexually active youths turn to perversions, alcohol, drugs, and, not infrequently, suicide.

Adolescents admitted to hospitals for depression have tripled, and suicide has increased by 200% since the establishment of school sex education --- that is in the past twenty or so years.

An epidemic of adolescent suicides is sweeping the United States. Teenage suicides now rank as the second leading cause of death in young people under twenty-one.

1972-1988
Here Lies Our Betsy

In the March 21, 1985 edition of the Los Angeles Jewish Community Bulletin, psychiatrist, Dr. Richard Bloom, reports that the dramatic rise in teen suicides can be directly attributed to the sex life of today's young adolescent.

Psychiatrist Bloom says, "Having extremely active sex lives by the time they're 14, teenagers have lost that feeling of looking forward to a special someone. Most kids have been through every kind of sexual experience by the time they're 16."

•

E. VALUES AND STANDARDS

Let's digress for a moment and take a look at the morality, values and standards that Planned Parenthood sponsored sex programs give junior and senior high school students.

The values and standards taught go out of their way to depreciate the values and morals of parents and the Judeo-Christian religions.

The conscience of an adult is the representative of moral demands made by the society in which he/she lives. We know it owes its origin to the identification with the parents. To the parents society has transferred the task of establishing ethical aims on the child and enforcing the restrictions upon instincts.

If parents are depreciated by the environment in the pre-adolescent or adolescent eyes, the youth's conscience already constructed by the parents is in danger of being lost or depreciated too: so that it cannot oppose instinctual impulses which press for satisfaction. The origin of many anti-social and character abnormalities can be explained in this way.

from *The Psychoanalytic Treatment of Children*

by Anna Freud

The consciences instilled in the minds of children by parents are decimated by the school sex programs.

Under the leadership of sex teachers, inexperienced youths are taught to set up their own values that, in fact, consist of having no values at all. Students are led to believe that values simply depend upon "enjoying what you do and do what you enjoy."

sex education

teacher's guide and resource manual

planned
parenthood
santa cruz
county

Should these statements about the values and standards promoted by sex educators seem exaggerated, an examination of any ordinary "sex education teacher's guide and resource manual" should be made --- as for example the manuals sponsored throughout the United States by Planned Parenthood and its related organizations.

Melvin Anchell, M.D., in a speech, "Sex in Schools," delivered at the Annual Session of the Medical Association of Georgia in May, 1972:

Clinical observations have shown that mature sexual adjustments fail to develop in individuals who frequently masturbated, lingered over childhood sexual excitements, or were involved in premature sexual activities. The sexual feelings of these patients are dominated by a need for masturbation and for deviant sex acts associated with a strong masochistic-sadistic element.

For example, in the Planned Parenthood teachers "Guide and Resource Manual" used in Santa Cruz, California,* (which is typical of the guides and manuals used throughout the United States), the "Sexuality and Values Section" consists entirely of three topics only.

(1) The first of these three topics is "Human Sexual Responses" which is based on the reports of 300 or so paid and unpaid volunteers and prostitutes used by Masters and Johnson to engage in sex acts while monitored by viewers and electronic devices.

(2) The second topic discussed in the "Sexuality and Values" section is Masturbation. The masturbation discussion consists of explaining and sanctioning all forms of masturbation that lead to orgastic emissions. If parents object to open masturbation, students are told to masturbate more privately in order to avoid family arguments.

*Available by sending $20.00 to Planned Parenthood, 212 Laurel Street, Santa Cruz, CA 95060.

(3) The final topic discussed in the "Sexuality and Values" section --- a section that is supposed to somehow give young people better values than established ones --- is Homosexuality. Homosexuality is taught as a normal variation, i.e., a normal lifestyle. The manuals advise sex teachers to bring homosexuals directly into the classroom to give students first hand information about how homosexuals conduct themselves sexually. Students are taught that the homosexual's oral-genital sex acts, his oral-anal acts, his self and mutual masturbation, etc., are normal and beneficial. The only prerequisite for engaging in homosexual-lesbian sex acts---students are taught---is that one enjoy them.

Recently, since AIDS has become a critical problem, one additional prerequisite has been added. Students are now taught to use latex condoms when engaging in some homosexual acts or when having sex with promiscuous partners.

Sodomy, however, is still regarded as a normal sexual practice that is equivalent to heterosexual genital intercourse.

Because of recent intensified demands from pro-homosexuals and homosexual activists, homosexuality and lesbianism are glorified in school classrooms more than ever.

Bennett went on to castigate the higher education community as morally hypocritical and intolerant: "Most of our colleges would not dream of claiming to offer a moral education to their students....But there is no shortage of moralizing and moral posturing-- especially the kind that does not cost anything of the individual, that does not take time or self-denial or effort." They have a "liberal bias," explicitly or implicitly censoring "unpopular [read conservative] ideas." This, Bennett claimed, flies in the face of the very academic freedom that professors are so quick to claim in defense of their left of center views.

Secretary of the Department of
Education, William Bennett.
(from *Education Update*,
American Heritage Foundation,
1986)

The sexual values and standards taught in Planned Parenthood sponsored sex programs have nothing to do with sexual morality.

The teachings are simply condonations of indifferent sex acts with indifferent sex partners, glorifications of perverts, approbation of masturbation and instructions in contraception and abortion.

FACT: "Planned Parenthood's youth activities amount, in effect, to a positive encouragement of sexual activity among teenagers. Showering these young people with contraceptives and provocative literature results in a tremendous peer pressure that makes teenagers who do not engage in sex feel abnormal. Planned Parenthood, like certain unscrupulous businesses, is creating a demand for its own services."

Facts About Planned Parenthood
By Paul Marx, Ph.D. and
Judie Brown

There is one main overriding theme in today's school sex programs --- and that theme is *carnality*. School sex teachings are essentially "how to" courses that condone and teach fornication along with all forms of perverted sex acts.

Among contributory forces working against perversions ... authoritative prohibition by society is a chief factor. Where homosexuality is not regarded as a crime it will be found in no small number of people.

Transformation of Puberty
by Sigmund Freud

Some teachers, for example, a sex teacher at Long Beach California State College, award extra credits to students who participate in perversions and report their perverted experiences openly in the classroom.

Such horrendous teachings not only create perverts out of some students, but an over-tolerance for perverts is instilled in the minds of all students.

This undue over-tolerance -- promoted as "understanding", "openness," and "frankness" -- destroys the natural mental defense mechanism to shun the pervert as a means of avoiding contamination. As a result students are left defenseless.

While this knowledge-based approach may seem reasonable to adults, research shows that, among children, knowledge-based drug education programs generally backfire by drawing too much attention to the drugs. Some programs that present detailed information on drugs, for instance, actually have increased the use of drugs "among curious teenagers." The fact is that normal children repeatedly exposed to a taboo activity, especially in the interesting ways suggested by the Education Department, tend to be drawn to that activity. Displaying different kinds of drugs, telling children how they are used, and detailing their effects stimulate children's interest. A 1971-1972 study of 935 students in several suburban Michigan junior high schools illustrates the dangers. After going through a drug curriculum that presented the facts about the physiology and pharmacology of drug use and its legal, social, and psychological ramifications, the students were found to be more likely to try drugs. The education program simply made them better informed drug users.*

"Education Update"
*American Heritage
Foundation,* 1986

*Sex education produces equivalent results.

Teaching youths an over-tolerance for perverts and an acceptance of the belief that orgasm achieved by any means is beneficial, can lead young people into becoming soulless polymorphous "mechanical robots" capable of engaging in any kind of sex act with indifference and without guilt. These are the characteristics of prostitutes and pimps.

School Based Health Clinics

Ed. Update: Is that how the clinics are advertised?

Brown: No. They are never advertised initially as having anything whatsoever to do with sexuality. They are promoted within communities as filling a need for total health and welfare services. It is said that these clinics will provide free physicals, and that children who are suffering from aches and pains of whatever nature will be able to come to the clinic for reliable on-campus medical services. The main argument against that, of course, is if that were truly the only purpose for the existence of a school-based health clinic, then what has the nurse been doing?

Ed. Update: What is the philosophy of health clinic proponents? What do they really want?

Brown: The goal of those who promote these clinics is to encourage children to be very mechanical about their sexuality. Rather than cherish our human sexuality as a gift, as something very unique about each and every one of us, children are encouraged to behave like animals. Setting aside all moral convictions, there is no provider of birth control for children today who warns them of the threat of pelvic inflammatory disease for the young girl who goes on the pill or the threat of AIDS for anybody who fools around outside of marriage.

It is very interesting to debate Dr. Laurie Zabin, author of the study of a Baltimore clinic, because she refuses to discuss the health aspects of the pill, or of promiscuity as it relates to venereal disease. She can only tout the two findings of her study. The first is that by having a sex clinic in the school the average teenager, according to anonymous questionnaires, delayed her first intercourse for seven months. The 13-year-old, in other words, waited until she was almost fourteen or the 15-year-old waited until she was almost sixteen. That is a victory according to Dr. Zabin. (Cont. to page 102)

Along with carnal teachings, the sex courses provide detailed information on contraception and abortion.

The other touted success is that the pregnancy rate decreased. The only reason the pregnancy rate decreased in the Baltimore study, the St. Paul Clinic study, or the Chicago Du Sable High School study is that they never counted abortions. In Maryland, for example, one-third of the abortions are performed on adolescent children, and yet the Baltimore study never mentions the word abortion because they do not figure terminated pregancies in the pregnancy count.

Ed. Update: Has the incidence of abortion risen in the past few years?

Brown: The teenage abortion rate has quadrupled since the inception of birth control information in the classroom (1970). We do not know how much higher the abortion rate will go with the existence of sex clinics in a given school because those who administer sex clinic programs always ignore abortion.

> from *The American Heritage*
> *Foundation:* "Education
> Update." 1986

Curbing Births, Not Pregnancies
By Stan E. Weed

More than a million teen-agers -- most of them unmarried --become pregnant each year, and the number is rising. The belief is widespread that the number will be reduced by opening more "family-planning" clinics and making them more accessible to teens. However, research a colleague and I have done suggests otherwise.

As the number and proportion of teen-age family-planning clinics increased, we observed a corresponding increase in the teen-age pregnancy and abortion rates: 50 to 120 more pregnancies per thousand clients, rather than the 200 to 300 fewer pregnancies as estimated by researchers at the Alan Guttmacher Institute (formerly the research arm of the Planned Parenthood Federation). We did find that greater teen-age participation in such clinics led to lower teen *birthrates*. However, the impact on the abortion and total pregnancy rates was exactly opposite the stated intentions of the program. The original problems appear to have grown worse.

Our research has been under way for two years, and analyzes date from such reliable sources as the Centers for Disease Control, the Guttmacher Institute, and U.S. Census data for all 50 states and the District of Columbia. Since pregnancy, abortion and birthrates also vary with such factors as urbanization, mobility, race and poverty, these variables were also taken into account for each state. Our findings have twice sustained formal review by specialists in the field.

(Mr. Weed is director of the independent Institute for Research and Evaluation in Salt Lake City. His two studies with Joseph A. Olsen cited here were published recently in the journal Family Perspective.)

The Wall Street Journal
Tuesday, October 14, 1986

As one student said, "if the clinic is giving it to you, it's telling you, 'Go ahead. Have sex.' Since they're giving it out, why not?"

The reduction in teen-pregnancy rates that is claimed as a result of the SBCs has been achieved by an increase in teen abortion, not by a reduction in teen sex activity."

Charles E. Rice,
Professor of Law,
Notre Dame University

It seems ludicrous, but after desensitizing the minds of students year after year to carnality, sex educators have the temerity to claim that their courses can prevent teen and preteen pregnancies if only the public would be even more supportive of school sex programs and school based "health clinics."

"Olga has an abortion to separate herself from her child in order to be free to work for the cause."

Genia undergoes an abortion without displaying the slightest sign of the normal feminine reaction to this experience. She has no time to give birth to a child or to love it.

So this is how the attitudes have been transformed in the past 30 years! Is this progress, and does this progress bring more freedom and potentialities of happiness to women--or is such freedom won at the price of inability to experience the most intense feminine happiness."

from *Psychology of Women*
by Helen Deutsch, M.D.

The callous persuasiveness used to teach students about abortions has so desensitized students to abortion that should a sexually educated girl become pregnant she submits to having these psychologically mutilating operations with about as much concern as having a manicure.

Indeed, to meet the demands of today's unwed teen pregnancies, abortion clinics have become as commonplace as beauty parlors.

"I have never seen a greater interest in *money* ... They are very good at getting their funds from a Congress seemingly enraptured by the pieties, pontifications, and poor-mouthings of higher education. But very few words can be heard from any of these representatives about ... purpose, quality, curriculum, the moral authority and responsibilites of universities."

> Secretary of the Depart-
> ment of Education
> William Bennett

FACT: Planned Parenthood receives charitable contributions from many chapters of the United Way and similar groups. In 1980 the organization's budget was about $140.8 million, at least $69.7 million of which was paid by the American Taxpayers.

> *Facts About Planned
> Parenthood -*
> by Paul Marx, Ph.D.
> and Judie Brown

The Allan Guttmacher Institute, a major activistic arm of Planned Parenthood, goes even further and places the blame for today's preteen and teen pregnancies on American manufacturers for not developing better contraceptives for sexually educated students.

The Guttmacher Institute and Planned Parenthood sex educators do not begin to place the blame on themselves for the sexual disasters in many of today's young people, but they point their fingers accusingly at parents and the U.S. Congress for not providing even more funds for their school sex programs.

NO. 78694528	United States Government **DEPARTMENT OF EDUCATION** Washington, D.C.	**AMOUNT:** $1,152,624.00
		GRANT DATE: 1979-81

Pay to the
Order of: Planned Parenthood, Feminist Press & NOW Legal Defense/Ed.

One million one hundred fifty-two thousand six hundred twenty four and 00/100

FACSIMILE

DOLLARS

Approved by: *Secretary of Education*
Secretary of Education

CF5R

Non-Negotiable Simulated Check

NO. 68427986	United States Government **DEPARTMENT OF LABOR** Washington, D.C.	**AMOUNT:** $640,000.00
		GRANT DATE: 1980-81

Pay to the
Order of: Gay and Lesbian Community Services Center

Six hundred forty thousand and 00/100

FACSIMILE

DOLLARS

Approved by: *Secretary of Labor*
(Secretary of Labor, CETA Division

CF5R

Non-Negotiable Simulated Check

NO. 58246921	United States Government **DEPARTMENT OF HEALTH & HUMAN SERVICES** Washington, D.C.	**AMOUNT:** $186,140.00
		GRANT DATE: 1979-80

Pay to the
Order of: New Ways Ministry & Center for Homosexual Eval. & Research

One hundred eighty-six thousand one hundred forty and 00/100

FACSIMILE

DOLLARS

Approved by: *Secretary of Health & Human Services*
Secretary of Health & Human Services

CF5R

Non-Negotiable Simulated Check

The fact is that the U.S. Planned Parenthood organization is so highly funded by American taxpayers that it is now aggressively attempting to spend some of their excess monies for promoting school sex programs and contraception-abortion "school based health clinics" into schools of other nations.

NEW STUDY: GOVERNMENT-FUNDED BIRTH CONTROL, SEX ED LEAD TO INCREASE IN TEENAGE PREGNANCIES

Providing taxpayer funded contraceptives and abortions to teenagers is leading to an increase, rather than a decrease, in teen pregnancies. So concludes a recently-released study by Professor Jacqueline Kasun, Ph.D., of Humboldt State University.

According to Dr. Kasun's spring 1986 report, entitled "Teenage Pregnancy: What Comparisons Among States and Countries Show," "comparisons among states and countries provide no support of the claim that government birth control can reduce pregnancy, ... considerable evidence that restrictions on access, especially in the form of requirements for parental consent, can reduce pregnancy."

Dr. Kasun's research reveals that there are large variations in teenage pregnancy rates and programs among the American states. What is interesting, the research said, is a state-by-state comparison of those statistics.

Dr. Kasun found that four states led the rest in 1980 for (1) providing free access to publicly-funded abortion and (2) having spent higher than the national average amounts per person on publicly-funded birth control. Those states are California, Hawaii, Georgia, and New York.

Those states do not require parental consent or notification for minors' contraceptives or abortions, and abortions are provided at public expense.

Rather than experiencing a reduction in the number of teen pregnancies and abortions, Dr. Kasun's research discovered that "all four states have higher-than-average teenage pregnancy rates as well as higher-than-average of teenage abortions-plus-unmarried births."

Statistical testing by the method of rank correlation showed that "states that spend relatively large amounts on government birth control also tend to have high rates of teenage abortions-plus-unmarried-births." Those states include Georgia, Vermont, South Carolina, and Tennessee. (Cont. to page 114)

Despite arguments to the contrary given by Planned Parenthood and sex educators, the fact is that there has been an ever increasing number of unwed preteen and teen pregnancies since public school sex programs and "school based health clinics" have come into existence.

Millions of teenagers become pregnant each year. In 1979, for example, it was determined that 5,000,000 adolescent girls between the ages of *fifteen and nineteen* engaged in sexual intercourse. One year later, in 1980, 1,100,000 pregnancies occurred in these 5,000,000 sexually active fifteen to nineteen year old girls. 460,000 of these pregnancies ended in abortions. This statistical information does not begin to include the number of pregnancies and abortions in the *ten to fourteen year old sexually educated girls.*

But those states which spent the least on birth control and abortions tended to have the lowest rates of abortions-plus-unmarried births. Those states include Utah, South Dakota, Idaho, and North Dakota.

Programs Create Problems

"It may be argued that state programs for the control of teenage pregnancy are responses to problems, not causes of them," states Kasun. "The facts, however, suggest that the programs create problems." The researcher uses the California experience as her case in point.

California has consistently spent more than twice as much as the national average on government birth control, cites Kasun. In FY 1971-73, the California State Office of Family Planning spent $4 million. But by 1983, spending had increased to where the state spent $95 million a year on contraceptives, sterilizations, and abortions.

During this period, "the teenage pregnancy rate in California rose to a level that was 30% above the national level, and the teenage abortion rate more than tripled, to a level that was 60% above the national level."

In 1981, almost 60% of teenage pregnancies in California were aborted, compared with 45% for the nation.

According to Dr. Kasun, California promoted and provided sex education at all grade levels during this period, sent pregnancy counselors into schools, and promoted contraceptives and abortions to teenagers at public expense without notifying parents.

Reduced assess means reduced pregnancies

Based on statistical evidence, Dr. Kasun also suggests that "there is additional evidence ... that unwanted teenage pregnancy may be reduced not by increasing teenagers' access to birth control but by restricting it."

To support her claim, Dr. Kasun points out that "during the 1970s, the state of South Dakota reduced its use of Title X family planning funds, and there occurred a reduction in teenage pregnancy."

Similarly, "in 1980 the state of Utah passed a law requiring parental consent for minors to be given birth control, and rates of pregnancy and abortion among girls 15-17 fell."

In 1981, the state of Minnesota passed a law requiring parents to be notified of minors' abortions.

"There ensued dramatic reductions in abortions, births, and pregnancies," states Kasun. "The teenage abortion rate fell by 20% between 1980 and 1983; the pregnancy rate by 16%, and the fertility rate by 13%."

And, "in 1984, an English court prohibited giving prescription contraceptives to girls under 16; there ensued a decrease in abortions among this age group."

Such statistics were unprecedented prior to today's sex education. Dr. C.A. Domz, in his article appearing in the *Medical Economics Magazine*, had it right when he said that one would require 20-20 ostrich vision to dismiss such statistics as coincidence.

The truth is --- "There are none so blind as those who will not see."

Nowhere do the sex educators make the slightest suggestion that their devastating sex programs rank among the greatest tragedies that our nation has ever endured and that their sex courses should be stopped. Nowhere do they explain why schools have summarily assumed the right to inculcate carnality into the minds of students while at the same time they disclaim any responsibility for upholding sexual morality.

At no time do the sex teachers remotely suggest that the *cure* for today's (1) teen pregnancies, (2) prostitution, (3) venereal diseases, (4) criminality, and (5) suicides necessitates that the educational system upholds the family and respects basic Judeo-Christian morality -- a morality that supports the struggle for existence, sustains civilized life and a morality that is in line with the great religions of the Far East -- and a morality, whose life sustaining nature is unequivocally substantiated by psychoanalytic observations.

C.A. Domz, M.D., "Doctors Against Pornography"
Medical Economics Magazine,

Physicians are treating more and more sick girls...performing more abortions and coping with a pandemic of venereal disease...From a medical standpoint, there is much to wonder about a [sexual] revolution that precipitates so much physical and mental suffering.

Paul Popenoe, ScD. (Director of The American Institute of Family Relations in an article, "A Contribution To The Dialogue On Sex Education," *Child and Family Magazine:*

Teachers from many parts of North America...declared that it seemed to them hardly worthwhile to try to teach high school youngsters about venereal diseases because they seemed so indifferent and defiant...venereal diseases represent a challenge not merely to medical science but to morality — if one dare use such an old-fashioned word.

Sexually Transmissible Organisms in Adolescent Girls

A sexually active 15-year-old girl is estimated to have a one in eight chance of acquiring acute pelvic inflammatory disease, ... major emphasis must be placed on the detection of potentially devastating sexually transmitted infections, particularly chlamydia and gonorrhea, while they are still asymptomatic...

The overall prevalence of six sexually transmissible organisms as related to sexual activity status...were all isolated significantly more frequently from sexually active girls than from virginal girls. *Neisseria gonorrhoeae* and *Trichomonas vaginalis* were isolated exclusively from sexually active girls.

from *Pediatrics*, April 1986
vol. 77, p. 488

The sex educators have either a mental block -- that is a strong repression -- or, for some reason, cannot see that their sex programs are largely responsible for the (1) pregnancies, (2) abortions, (3) prostitution, (4) perversion, (5) suicides and (6) psychological, as well as, physical venereal diseases that are epidemic in today's youths.

The sex educators not only deny their accountability, but some rashly blame parents -- rather than themselves -- for the pregnancies, gutter sex and venereal diseases that are rife among many young people today.

Indeed, many sex educators portray themselves as saviors of youths by professing to protect students from the outmoded established standards and values of parents whose sexualities, the sex educators say, have been stunted by anachronistic morals and religion.

During the past 14 years, Planned Parenthood and its allies have hoodwinked legislators and bureaucrats into thinking that parental involvement will only exacerbate teen pregnancy rather than relieve it. Something as serious as this, so they say, should be left to the doctor and patient exclusively. Parents need not apply.

Time and events have proved them wrong. In Minnesota, where a 1981 law required parental notification for abortion, the pregnancy, abortion and birth rates among adolescents plummeted. According to a 1985 report by the House Select Committee on Children, Youth and Families, from 1980 to 1983, abortions to Minnesota teens, 15-19, dropped 40 percent; the teen birth rate decreased 23.4 percent and pregnancies decreased 32 percent. In the same period, the number of teens, 15-19, decreased by only 13.5 percent.

A similar trend in England was reported following a 1984 court case making it illegal for doctors to prescribe contraceptives to minors without parental consent.

"Focus: Contraceptives
for Children, A Parental
Control Battle"
by Senator Jesse Helms

All too frequently, some parents are persuaded to relinquish their own sensibilities in deference to the sex teachers.

Such parents are led to believe that "teacher knows best," and many of these mothers and fathers become zealous advocates for public school sex programs.

TIDBITS....

Up to 600,000 children under the age of 16 are engaged in prostitution. Between 300,00 and 600,00 children younger than 16 years old are used in child pornography, appearing in more than 264 publications.

from *CDL Reporter*

Recently*, a Chicago newspaper reported that 80% of the freshman to senior female enrollment in a Chicago high school were pregnant.

*1988

The national sexual calamity among many of our youths remains unabated.

The question is -- have the teachings of the sex educators and the influence of the pornographic entertainment media so thoroughly persuaded the public to accept preteen - teen sex, free love and perversions that they have already brought our nation to the "point of no return"?

F. WHAT CAN BE DONE?

Assuming that this point has not been reached, what can be done?

First, I believe the sexually gangrenous material filling the minds of young people as a result of today's sex education and the pornographic entertainment media must stop forming. A tourniquet preventing further spread of contamination is urgently needed.

Planned Parenthood type sex educators must be led to know that we have had enough.

Local, state and national school officials must be led to know that we expect them to translate our outrage into educational courses that serve the needs of civilized people! -- Not the needs of unrestrained barbarians.

There can be no compromise -- free love and perversions promoted by school sex programs cannot exist side by side with mature love and family life. Each destroys the other.

In conclusion, two matters stand out:

-- The first is that for the continued existence of *life sustaining sex* which completely depends upon "affectionate, monogamous, man/woman, long lasting love relationship," it is as necessary to eradicate today's "psychological sexual diseases" as it is to eradicate today's physical sexual diseases such as AIDS.

--And secondly for the survival of a civilization based on families composed of individuals living by consciences instead of barbarians living by instincts only -- it is essential that sexual decency be maintained, not only in our homes, but also in the schools to which we send our children.

In our social structure built up over hundreds of years, the family constitutes the individual's first environment . . . .

Cultural factors can, nevertheless, be so powerful that they extensively modify human behavior.

Psychology of Women
Helene Deutsch, M.D.

G. NOTES, FACTS: AND AFTERTHOUGHTS

I. EPILOGUE

The author upholds no claim for the originality of the facts in this book. The information presented is based on established psychoanalytic precepts that have been repeatedly substantiated by clinical observations. However, psychoanalytic precepts alone were not all that was relied upon. Materials from various sources, other psychological systems and published case histories were used when these stood the acid-test of scientific clinical evaluation and were of value to the patient.

Popular entrancement with data presented by today's sexperts have led many leaders in society to reserve the term "scientific" for data obtained from laboratory gadgeteering, statistical-questionnaires and scholasticals. Tremendous weight, often in excess of their importance, is now commonly placed on the findings from such procedures. These methods, when used by institutional professors, academecians and statisticians to learn about human sexuality, produce findings that are usually far removed from sexual truth as it relates to mankind.

For the physician the quintessence of psychological truths is obtained from the "clinical approach."

The great value of psychoanalysis, which requires a one-to-one relationship between patient and physician, is that it provides insight into the dynamics of human nature and directly attacks the question: "Why do people act that way?"

(Note: There is a great difference between psychoanalysis and psychiatry. Psychiatry is basically a descriptive and classificatory science. Its orientation is toward physical explanations and treatments of mental and emotional phenomena. Psychoanalysis is a science in which understanding of people comes first and classifications and prescribing medications for emotional disorders are second.)

"Psychoanalytic investigation considers that entire mental and emotional nature of humans. It is the only means of acquiring overall information concerning human sexuality.

Institutional laboratory experiments patterned after bordellos and statistical-questionnaire tests mathematically analyzed are methods used by academician sex experts to measure sexual behavior, motives and feelings. Findings resulting from such investigations all too frequently lead the non-clinical investigators into making erroneous assumptions that are then popularized as scientific truths.*

The clincial approach to the dynamics of human sexuality involves the whole person. Such study is time-consuming but through careful observations much insight into the behavior of man is gained.

Data accumulated by clinicians is as scientific as that collected by biologists and chemists. There are, however, those who say that psychoanalytic methods are unscientific. To paraphrase psychiatrist Stanley Cobb "One need not bother with the intellectual snobs who would keep the term 'science' for laboratory 'gadgeteering'."[1]

Consider experiments conducted by Masters, W.A. and Johnson, N.E.

[1] Anchell, Melvin, M.D., *A Second Look At Sex Education,* Educulture Inc., Publishers, 1972.

"No book, no journal and no refresher course can teach a doctor so well as the critical study of his own patients."

I.R. McWhinney
(*British Medical Journal*)

II. BIBLIOGRAPHY

The reading of this book has not been interrupted by frequent footnotes and I offer no exhaustive bibliography. For those who are unbiased, their inborn sensitivities will measure the truth of what has been said. For those who have been persuaded by the opinions of pro-sex educationists, it is unlikely that a bibliography will change their minds.

The information for my expertise has been obtained eclectically from over 40 years of critical, conscientious clinical involvement -with men, women and children; young and old. Since 1967 and currently, I have spoken before concerned parents, appeared before school boards and testified as an expert witness in various courts about the, adverse effects that Planned-Parenthood-type sex education programs have on youth and on the Nation.

III. SOURCES

Copies of the literature, reports, sketches, tapes and other accoutrements used by Planned Parenthood oriented educators in their sex courses are not easily obtained. Parents or interested individuals requesting such information are usually greeted courteously by the teachers and the school librarians. Reams of material may be given to satisfy a request, but when these things are examined they are found to be far removed from what is actually taught in the sex classrooms.

Parents may be invited to visit the sex classes, but when present sexual ambience changes in the classroom. The parent gets the feeling that he/she is a snooper and that his/her presence is an unappreciated imposition. Few individuals who attend the sex classes to acquire firsthand information will return for further visits.

If bona fide information regarding what goes on in the sex classrooms is needed, one should obtain a copy of a Planned Parenthood's *Sex Education Teacher's Guide and Resource Manual*.

Copies of such a manual should be available from Planned Parenthood of Monterey, California. On the following pages are replicas of the order forms that are in the back of the *Sex Education Teacher's Guide and Resource Manual* published by Planned Parenthood Santa Cruz County, California.

The first duplicated order form is for the Sex Teacher's *Guide and Resource Manual*. The second order form is for *Peer Education*. The latter is a mirror image of the *Teacher's Guide and Manual*. However, the "teachers" using *Peer Education* are school students.

143

ORDER BLANK

PLANNED PARENTHOOD OF SANTA CRUZ COUNTY
212 Laurel Street
Santa Cruz, CA 95060   Date_____

Please send _____ copy(ies) of **SEX EDUCATION: TEACHER'S GUIDE AND RESOURCE MANUAL** @ $15.00 plus $2.00 shipping and handling to:

Please Print:

NAME _____

STREET _____

CITY, STATE, ZIP_____

SIGNATURE _____

_____Check or money order enclosed   _____Please bill me
      (No cash please)

PLANNED PARENTHOOD OF MONTEREY COUNTY
5 Via Joaquin
Monterey, CA 93940   Date_____

Please send _____ copy(ies) of **PEER EDUCATION** -- an adolescent sex education program at $15.00. This includes shipping and handling.

Please print:

NAME _____

STREET _____

CITY, STATE, ZIP_____

SIGNATURE _____

_____Check or money order   _____Please bill me
      (No cash, please)

144

By using peers to teach the sex programs, sex educators speculate that students will be more receptive to the sex instructions.

A criteria used for selecting a student to teach sex is that he/she must be of a masterful nature -- a leader of other students. Parental consent is, also, required. The student sex teacher is given brief instructions in how to conduct the sex class; after which he espouses the prescribed sex doctrines to fellow students in the classroom.

NOTE: In the foregoing manuals one will find:

A. A series of psychological teaching techniques designed to intensely and thoroughly effect a radical transformation in the beliefs and mental attitudes of the students.

B. Some of the brainwashing ploys are:

   1. BRAINSTORMING
   2. QUESTION AND ANSWER CARDS
   3. SEX FILMS--OF THE XXX RATED VARIETY
   4. CASE STUDIES
   5. ROLE PLAYING
   6. POPULAR HARD ROCK SEX MUSIC
   7. GRAFFITI BOARDS
   8. "UNCLE HENRY'S ADVICE COLUMN"
   9. VALUE CONTINUUMS
  10. AMBIGUOUS QUESTIONS, AND
  11. THE "ALLIGATOR RIVER STORY"

IV. HUMANOIDAL SEX and SEX EDUCATION

What is "normal"? The degree of mental health is not determined by an absence of inner personal conflicts but by the way these opposing emotional interests, ideas, etc. are reconciled.

"Abnormal" often represents a misrepresentation — a perversion — of what is "normal". Unfaithful, deformed reproductions of normal life are currently being spread by perverted minds. Sick themselves, these purveyors are making the abnormal appear normal.

As a physician I regard any behavior that supports life and allows death to occur from natural causes as normal. Behavior that leads to the destruction of life is abnormal.

The psychological venereal diseases spread by today's sex education interferences and the pornographic entertainment media are destructive to life and as such must be considered as societal abnormalities.

Sexual morality which has evolved from mankind's earliest beginnings is essential for life. Mature sexuality along with its associated sexual morals are antidotes to death instincts. Nowhere in today's popular school sex programs is mature sexuality and sexual morality emphasized.

The sexually emancipated-sexually aggressive females who are depicted as normal in movies, current novels and in sex education classes are not examples of social progress but, instead, are examples of social regression. They exemplify females possessed by tremendous inner turmoil; females who are in conflict with their natural femininity. Such women are not liberated and free individuals but are slaves to the demands of the culture in which they live. When the environment upholds sexual morality, woman's psyche requires that she act with sexual discretion. When the culture in which she lives condones free love, her psyche causes her to assume to some degree the characteristics of a loose woman. Uninhibited sex life is contrary to women's inner feminine nature. In truth, the sexually uninhibited woman is an artifact that is produced, sometimes, by a woman's desire to prove herself totally independent or, more frequently, by fantasies arising from man's erotic desires.

Many of todays sexually aggressive females have foregone the ultimate feminine needs of marriage and family life, motherhood and of loving and being loved. Some attempt to satisfy love needs entirely through acts of copulation. However, these impoverished women derive no real pleasure from the sex act. Many such females are products of premature sexual activity brought about by sex education and the demands made upon them by a sexually pseudo-liberated society.

Not only do popular sexual attitudes destroy the lives of some women, but the lives of many men have been torn apart by the current 'sexual revolution'.

Some males, who regard free love as a modern day bonanza, aid and abet the state of sexual confusion in promiscuous females. Impressed by sexperts, many men and women regard the sex act as a cure for all mental tensions. This false teaching has been further perpetuated by an ever increasing number of sexperts.

The argument that the normalcy of today's common sexual practices is proven by their evident prolificacy is as logical as claiming that the bubonic plague in the 15th century was normal because so many people at that time had the disease.

There is one inexorable law in Nature: "When the sexual instincts are perverted, the death instincts take over."

The foregoing discourse leads me to believe that the sex education ideas and opinions of a leading spokesman for sex educators are grossly abnormal. This sex education spokesman, Albert Ellis, has helped fashion today's sex education. He was a main speaker at the American Association of Sex Educators and Counselors and Therapists (AASEC) meeting held in Washington D.C., March 1972. The following excerpts of his AASEC speech are taken from the Barbara Morris Report, April 1972:

QUOTING ALBERT ELLIS

"We are now starting planned biology...seeing that certain individuals would better not be born ... Planned biology will plan happiness...having a f-king good time on earth rather than getting into heaven and getting on the right hand of God. -----------.

It is a 'quaint notion' that women have children by their husbands.... We will have sperm banks so we can have Leonardo Da Vincis of our choice ... We may louse up the system and kill ourselves...but we will end up with happier results.

The goal of most human beings is an ego trip — to show you are a worthwhile human being ... Then they have a heavenly goal — 99 out of 100 have this goal — to be better than others on earth and holier than thou in heaven ... They don't accept humanism — that I will never be anything than human. They have to be taught to be human — f-ked-up and human.

Culture in the future will be based on reality — no spiritual, mystical humanity. If you accept infallible f-ked-up humanity, we will have a better culture and sex education."

In my opinion, Ellis's advice to sex teachers is abnormal. His remark "We may louse up the system and kill ourselves --- but we will end up with happier results." is only half true - the first half.

In 1972, the sensibilities of normal people were appalled by such egregious recommendations for teaching sex education. But since then the culture has been immersed in an environment rife with pornography and obscenity. To add to the confusion decisions handed down by courts uphold the "rights" of pornographers and perverts.

Ellis and his followers have managed to persuade a great many people. By their repeated sexual promulgations they have desensitized innumberable minds to sexual vulgarity. What is normal is no longer generally accepted. And, what is abnormal has become "normal". Few people can remain totally immune to the incessant bombardment from pornographers, affluent sex educators and aggressive homosexual activists.

Walter Bernard, PhD., Asst. Prof. of Psychology,
Long Island University, from the *New York Times*:

"The avalanche of pornography floods the consciousness with sex to a far greater extent than it should be. It thus deprives the mind of the time and interest needed for other aspects of consciousness, other areas of interest basic to a well-rounded wholesome life. In psychology this is a problem of "mental hygiene." Sex, a powerful drive, hardly needs any stimulation. It obtrudes itself frequently upon consciousness without outward "help." "

V. CHICKENS?

The idea that children should be taught sex in schools was first introduced in the late sixties. My first knowledge of such an idea came on the occasion of completing a series of lectures at a local university on "affectionate love". After my talks a professor asked me if I knew Mary Calderone. The name was not familiar to me. The professor went on to explain that Mary Calderone was a doctor who had graduated from medical school rather late in life — around the age of 50. She had never been involved in clinical medicine, but did have a position with a public health agency. Dr. Calderone, the professor said, had lectured at the University the previous day. The purpose of her speech was to convince the education students that it was essential to teach young children about sex.

Calderone had stopped at the University on her way around the country. She spoke wherever possible in a determined effort to get her sex education ideas popularized. In her talks she showed models of chickens mating. She explained that such models offered a good way to teach young children about sex.

Shortly after I learned of Mary Calderone and her organization, Sex Information and Education Counsel of the United States, their names began to appear everywhere.

Mary Calderone—SIECUS were, to my knowledge, the originators of public school sex education in the United States. They were phenomenally successful. It took Calderone—SIECUS only a few short years to propel their sex education programs into public schools throughout the nation.

Once Calderone—SIECUS established a firm beach head, they stepped back and largely passed their sex education plans onto Planned Parenthood with its associated agencies.

Quoting Mary S. Calderone, M.D., Executive Director of the Sex Information and Education Council of the United States (SIECUS):

"You can't go into sex education with a preconceived idea that you will teach sex education in order to promote morality. You have to give young people knowledge, and then kids will promote their own morality."

Max Levin, M.D., Psychiatrist, New York Medical College:

But, sadly, many of our sex educators, even among those who are highly respected, seem (in my opinion) to be confused and they are leading our youngsters astray. I disagree with the SIECUS position that sex education 'must not be moral indoctrination'...I speak not as a clergyman but as a psychiatrist. There cannot be emotional health in the absence of high moral standards and a sense of human and social responsibility. I know that today morality is a 'dirty word' but we must help our youth to see that moral codes have meaning beyond theology; they have psychological and sociological meaning.

Calderone—SIECUS—Planned Parenthood have saturated public schools with sex education. They have never been effectively stopped. Once one of CSP's representatives appears before a school board, the board members seem to become mesmerized and sex education programs in that school become a fait accompli.

Countless concerned parents and citizens groups have formed to stop the roaring CSP juggernaut; but the success of the CSP sex education team keeps rolling along.

151

Sex education has come a long way since I first heard about Mary Calderone and her chickens. "What comes first: the chicken or the egg?"

How many parents old enough to have sons and daughters in high schools can remember encountering the sexual abuses so common in today's sex educated young people.

There is no doubt about what came first. Sexual degeneracy rapidly follows the public school sex programs. Bombed by the sexual gutter-fantasies in the entertainment media and the authoritatively presented pornography in school sex classes, the base sexual instincts of sexually overstuffed youths have exploded.

In retrospect, the only NATURAL remnant that remains from Mary Calderone's beginning sex teachings are the copulating chickens.

VI. A BRIEF LOOK

A glimpse of a typical 'Family Life Education' program can be obtained from the outline of Planned Parenthood's sex education curriculum for New England.

PLANNED PARENTHOOD'S
FAMILY LIFE EDUCATION CURRICULUM K-12
of Northern New England
by Sal Wiggin

SETTING THE FOUNDATION . . . . gives a detailed account of how to win support in the community and *discourage opposition groups, i.e.* "Right To Life," etc.

KINDERGARTEN . . . . P. 5—Children are asked to outline partner's bodies and verbally label all parts including genitals and buttocks. Ten pages on Personal Safety primarily dealing with prevention of child abuse.

GRADE 1 . . . . P. 5—Children are read "The True Story of Where Babies Come From," by Per Holm Knudson. Then they are asked to "illustrate" where babies come from. Also asked to talk about feelings.

GRADE 2 . . . . Review where babies come from. Examine types of families. Read poems about sex sterotyping things people do. Discuss the book: "Free To Be.. You And Me," by Marlo Thomas. "My Dog The Plumber"—p. 87.

GRADE 3 . . . . P. 11 & 12—Diagrams shown of Male/Female reproductive Systems. Children are asked to make models of reproductive organs using: Ping Pong Balls, straw, paper cup, yarn and cellophane bag. P. 11—"One sperm enters the egg and this begins a baby. The fertilized egg (zygote) must now attach to the inside wall of the uterus for the baby to grow."
Prenatal stages of development are briefly outlined.

GRADE 4 . . . . P. 6—"Two physically mature (teenager or adult) people, a male and female, are necessary ingredients" for intercourse. The children are asked to describe the sexual act, chromosomes and the fertilization process. "How I Was Born" Nielson, Lennart.

Under Grade 4--There are three more pages on personal safety for Kindergarten. There are 28 pages on Personal Safety for Grades 1—3. There are 25 pages on Personal Safety for Grades 4—6. Pages 7 & 8—Prenatal stages of development are briefly mentioned.

GRADE 5 . . . . P. 7—Pathways of sperm and egg are explained. P. 11-16—Menstruation and reproductive functions of M/F are described. P. 12—"If a female does not want to be pregnant, she can either not have sex or use birth control when she does."

GRADE 6 . . . . P. 12—"Dear Diary" movie shown. Question: What was "the gushy feeling down there?" "What are some causes of the tingly feelings in the vulva region?" "Do girls masturbate?" P. 13—"Masturbation is a normal activity for males and females of all ages. It means touching, caressing, stimulating ones genitals... Masturbation is one of the earliest and most effective ways children learn about their bodies. It is one of the initial treatments for adults having sexual problems. Adults are taught to masturbate. Naturalness and normalcy about masturbation are helpful attitudes to express to children to enhance positive sexual development. Now most pediatricians are encouraging parents to allow children the privacy to masturbate. There are many people that believe that masturbation is harmful and abnormal. This belief is not supported by facts.
P. 15-16—Review of sexual organs and their functions.

GRADE 7 . . . . P. 1-7—Changing family roles and respon-sibilities throughout our society. P. 2—"The role of the parents are more interchangeable now. Neither parent is locked into a particular function or role." P. 11—"Imagine that you will be seeing a doctor or health professional. Make a list of questions you have about your personal health and development." P. 23—Ex. of a Dating Continuum: Learners are asked to define each one: Friends—Dating—Pre-engagement—Engaged, Living Together. (No Mention of Marriage.) P. 24—Children presented with "Dear Abby" letters and are asked to give advice. Discussion about values and beliefs. *Grades 7 & 8—Twelve pages on "Personal Safety."*

GRADE 8 . . . . P. 13—Handout: "Am I Pregnant?". Discuss how pregnancy occurs. Film showing fertilization and pregnancy called "Beginning of Life."
P. 14 & 15—"Once fertilization occurs, there are still many important occurrences before pregnancy can result." "Implantation occurs on the seventh or eighth day and is completed on the 12th day."
P. 16—In the first mention of pregnancy, the first trimester of fetal development is ignored: "After the first trimester, or 12 weeks, the embryo has begun developing the major organ systems and is called a fetus." P. 16—"After birth it is called a neonate, at two weeks old doctors call it an infant."
P. 18—Minimal outline of prenatal development. In third trimester they state "body proportions are more human." "Fetus can survive...if born prematurely." They do not state that babies born earlier than third trimester have also survived.
P. 20-1—Student is to identify: when in one's life contraception may be appropriate for him or her; discuss and clarify myths about contraception, and list five methods of contraception and how to obtain each one. Two recommended films are "Making Decisions About Sex" and "Are You Ready For Sex?"
P. 21—"Getting Contraceptive Supplies before ever having intercourse is a way to protect one's self."
P. 22—A listing of different types of contraceptives, inc.

155

vasectomy and tubal ligation.

P. 23—"Prescriptive and non-prescriptive contraceptives are available at Planned Parenthood offices, cheaper than drug stores."

P. 37—Discuss reasons why or why not to have sex at this age.

P. 39—Using a diagram entitled "INTERCOURSE," all possible methods of contraception are listed under "Mutual Responsibility," inc. tubal ligation and vasectomy. The other two headings to "Not contracept" and "To Not Have" (intercourse) are not listed under "Mutual Responsibility." Listed options under "To Not Have" are Erotic Movies and Literature, Masturbation and sexual fantasies.

REPRODUCTIVE HEALTH - GRADES 9-12

P. 1—"Physical and emotional functioning are linked more than text books and health care providers ever mention. P. 2—Male Anatomy test and filmstrip on "Anatomy Attitudes."

P. 5-15—Ten pages on Male Anatomy and Physiology.

P. 8—Vasectomy.

P. 16-29—Thirteen pages on Female anatomy and sexual health care.

P. 17—View filmstrip, "Anatomy & Attitudes," and female anatomy test.

P. 28—COMMUNITY RESOURCE SHEET handed out. Students asked to investigate at least five resources for community services such as: Pregnancy tests and counseling — abortion services — contraceptive care and supplies.

P. 42—"Birth control is an option for people who choose to be sexually active but do not want to be pregnant. About half of all high school students are sexually active…"

P. 43—"How do you begin a conversation about birth control within a dating relationship?" No one can say when the "right" time is, although many would suggest it is at marriage." "What do you think your parents values are?"

P. 44—"If people are not sexually active, should they have birth control just in case?" Pamphlet given "Deciding About Birth Control" Contraceptives are passed around for "Hands On Opportunity."

**P. 45—"Learners asked to write 3-5 page paper about method of birth control most appropriate for them at this stage of their lives."

P. 46-54—Eight pages describing birth control methods available; advantages and disadvantages, (inc. vasectomy and tubal ligation). P. 47-54—Natural methods of birth control are not discussed at length "because of the variety of guidelines available" for this information. All other artificial methods are discussed at length. (p. 48).

P. 73-74—Stages of fetal development: minimal outline. (Grade 8 p. 15 "Implantation occurs on 7-8th day after fertilization.")

**P. 73—WHICH IS CORRECT????

In "D" section the developing baby is referred to as a blastocyst until implantation, then as an embryo until seventh week, then as a fetus. (Grade 8 — p. 16 — After 12 weeks, the embryo is called a fetus.)

In "E" section it is stated that at the fourth week of pregnancy, the blastocyst implants itself in uterus; at the beginning of the fifth week the fertilized egg is now an embryo.

P. 74—(6th week) "Human embryo looks like a pig, rabbit, chicken or elephant embryo." "End of 5th month, if born, may live a few minutes, but very rare." "End of 6th month, if born may live several hours or days. One in ten survive." "End of 7th month, 50% chance of survival." "End of 8th month, 90% chance of survival."

P. 81—"Learners will clarify and express values about adoption, abortion and teenage pregnancy." Next seven pages about "learning activities" concerning the subjects above. "Facts about Early Abortion" and "Where Do You Stand?" are handouts.

P. 84—Recommended resource: "Ambivilance about Abortion" by Linda Franks. Explanation of higher death rate among babies born to teenagers.

P. 86—"Statistics show the effect of having a baby on a teenager's life are generally negative."

**P. 89—"Would I make a good parent?" questionnaire. "Could I accept a child that was physically or mentally abnormal?" "Have I had experience with children of all ages?" "Would I expect my child to take care of me in my old age?" List the five most important things or qualities a person should have to be a good parent.

P. 92— ???? "Before Abortion was legalized, an estimated 700,000 women a year obtained illegal abortions." "Aristotle wrote that it should be available to women with sufficient children. Plato felt it should be mandatory for women over 40 or victims of incest."

P. 94—*Abortion Methods* used today are led, including "vacuum aspiration...frequently done without confirmation of pregnancy by urine test...DES There is a great deal of concern about DES." (Above) "In the third trimester (after 26 weeks), the fetus becomes "viable" capable of life outside the womb..." This is *inaccurate* as the fetus is "viable" as early as twenty weeks (5 months).

P. 95—"Legal abortion is a relatively safe, uncomplicated procedure. Abortion in the first trimester is 10 times safer than childbirth... There is concern that repeated abortions may make it more difficult for a woman to carry pregnancy to term." Results are quoted from a survey done by a national abortion group indicating that 83% of American voters supported abortion in all or some circumstances.

*** P. 96—"When does fetus become a person?" "The main issue is the question of whether the woman's right to control her own body and choose an abortion overrides the right of the fetus to develop and be born."

P. 98—"Complications are possible with early abortion, as with any kind of surgery; but even the ones most likely to occur are encountered in only a small number of cases." (Back of) P. 98: "At this point there is no clear evidence that one early abortion carries any risk to future pregnancies." "Emotional problems after abortion are uncommon, and when they happen they usually go away quickly."

P. 99—"WHERE DO YOU STAND?" questionnaire. Some of the questions are: "Should abortions be legal?" "Who should pay the cost of Abortion?" "When does life begin?" "Should parents pass a test to be allowed to become parents?"

* * * *Should parents pass a test to be allowed to become parents?"*

INTERPERSONAL RELATIONSHIPS—GRADES 9-12

P. 5—"Our society has been eroding many same-sex relationships in favor of a series of dating relationships. Through same-sex relationships we learn some very important skills that are essential to the survival of interpersonal relationships."

P. 12—Students are asked to role-play a specified situation. The instructor is to "guide the discussion toward setting up some criteria for making a choice between the values of single-sex and other-sex friendships.

P. 14—"Divide group into same sex-groups and have each group list the activities they enjoy sharing with members of their own sex. Develop another list of special/important things males learn from males and females learn from females. (They are not put into groups of opposite sex and asked to do these things.)

P. 15 & 19—Shown Filmstrip "Four Sequences" Same Sex Relationship Sequence:

Some of the frames of the film are...

"Close up of adult males with arms around each other"

"Close up of young adult girls kissing" "Girls nude bathing together"

"Girls comparing breast size" "Nude boys relaxing on patio" "Teenage boys reading Playboy"

"Adult males in shower" "Close ups of Adult Males

kissing"

****"A chart shown on the incidence of bisexualtiy"

P. 15—"The purpose of this exercise is to illustrate that touch, affection and intimacy between members of the same sex are natural aspects of important learning experiences for those involved." Student is to think of one's best friend of the same sex and to imagine that on the given sheet that the printed drawings are of their best friend. They are then to "shade in the parts of the friend's body they would feel comfortable touching, depending whether they were in a public or private setting."

*** P. 17—"It is important for adults to be aware that the normal pattern of psychosexual development for children and young people moves from solitary masturbatory behavior to masturbation with one or two friends of the same sex to exploratory sexual behavior with them."

P. 18—"In general our society does not consider homosexuality acceptable, although the medical and psychiatric communities do not find any indication that this is abnormal."

P. ?—"The important factor is that they develop relationships with friends. This more than dating, can adequately prepare them for loving adult relationships."

P. 27—"Dating serves a variety of purposes. The following is a capsulation of its functions:
1. Recreation; 2. Companionship; 3. Personal & Social growth; 4. A means of sexual experimentation or exploitation.
About 50% of high school seniors are sexually active, as are 70% of unmarried 19-year-olds."

P. 39—"Have learners fill out values questionnaire individually and discuss in large group." "Discuss role of sexual activity within adolescent dating relationship for intercourse to occur." "Fill out (hand out) 'Expressing Physical Affection'" "View a film about sexual activity within a dating relationship." "The Date" — Little Red Schoolhouse. Handout: "Are You Ready

For Sex?"

P. 54—2 films, 2 slides: Recommended to explore the effects of sex role types. 4 references to reading material on this subject.

P. 56—Discussion of different societies with different roles for men and women than what we have in our society. "What are advantages and disadvantages of traditional roles?"

"Because of their role as protector and provider, men are expected to make the big decisions...in family matters. This excessive sense of responsibility severely stiffles men from being themselves..."

P. 59-62—4 pages of questions on sex role stereotyping.

P. 1—Learners are asked to fill out "Parenthood Questionnaire" (on P. 12). The Instructor supplement to this questionnaire gives "helpful comments to augment discussion:"

"1. Ann Lander's and Redbook studies have shown that people in marriage report they are happier than couples involved in marriages with children.

"11. Popular myth suggests that humans, especially female, have an instinctive drive to have children. There is no scientific confirmation of this fact."

"16. Overpopulation is of great concern throughout the world. While it may not personally affect us today, it will greatly impact on us and our children in the future. But in less developed countries overpopulation is a severe problem. It is important to conserve natural resources now, than to wait until they are almost depleted."

P. 1—Students asked to complete "Are You Ready?" (on P. 13). Purpose: Questions asked to identify attitudes and skills needed for parenthood: (Some of the questions are listed below)...

"Have you ever cleaned a child's cuts or scratches? Are you prepared to?" "Have you ever experienced financial hardships as a result of supporting a child? Are you prepared to?" "Have you ever attended to a crying child? Are you prepared to?"

P. 2—"Invite a person or couple that has chosen not to parent to address the group on the decision not to parent." It is not suggested that someone who has children be invited to address the group.

Learners are to investigate alternatives to parenthood that continue an involvement with children; i.e., foster care, group leader for youths, adult volunteer programs within community.

Learners are asked to write a five page paper on "pros and cons of parenthood considering their personal skills and experience, the 'if' of parenthood for them and the 'when' if appropriate," including "ramifications of their decision on their future social and family relationships as well as their ability to achieve their personal goals."

P. 37—Frequently other adults appear to have more successful communication with adolescents than parents. It is important for adolescents to understand that they can and should be expanding their support system and tapping resources that can assist them to meet their needs, i.e., guidance counselor, social worker, family therapists, etc.

P. 41—Divorce..."is optional, but it is assumed that most people will experience it during some part of their life."

"By 1980, only 43% of people agreed with this statement, "all married couples who can, ought to have children. This suggests that parenthood is now being considered an option rather than a necessity of adult life."

P. 44—"Probably, the most important decision is that of whether or not to parent. Tasks include:

Risking pregnancy and childbirth. —
Accommodating to the parental role.
Learning to relate emotionally to offspring. —
Locating competent child care as appropriate.

162

SELECTING RESOURCES

P. 7—"One theme presented in the Family Life Curriculum is the gradual shift of responsibility for a child's or young adult's health care from the parents to the individual her/himself."

P. 9—"Teachers and administrators can be prepared to diffuse controversy by relying on a printed selection policy and a thorough knowledge of the materials used in the program."

P. 4—(Policies and Procedures For Selection of Instructional Materials.) "In the event that materials are questioned, the principles of freedom to read, the right to access of materials and the integrity of the professional instructional staff must be defended rather than the materials."

In this family life curriculum, individual masturbation and masturbation with partners, homosexuality, use of contraceptives, abortion, and zero population growth are highly endorsed. Students are continually directed toward outside sources to find answers to their questions or problems. Not once during the entire (900?) page curriculum it seems obmissive not to have a section devoted to marriage. Also, it is implied that interested people be required to pass a test to be allowed to be a parent--that first they should have had a variety of listed experiences with children.(sic)

A BRIEF LOOK AT
ONE MORE EXAMPLE:

Material from sex course offered to Seventh, Eighth and Ninth grade children in Howell, Michigan:*

The man has something that we call a penis. It is something like a finger and it hangs in front of his body between his legs. Most of the time it hangs there quite loosely. But, when he is attracted to his wife in love, then the penis becomes hard and firm and it stands erect, kind of at right angles with the rest of his body. And this happens so that it will be able to fit easily into a special place in a woman's body that was made for it. This special place in a woman's body we call the vagina. It's an opening between her legs. And when she wants him to show her that he loves her, the vagina becomes kind of wet and slippery so that it will be easy for the penis to enter it....the penis moves back and forth inside the vagina until from the end of the penis there comes a kind of milky fluid and we call this, when this happens, we say that the man is having an ejaculation. And this makes the man feel real good. And the woman, too....she feels good all over, too.

As for the creams, foams, and sprays, they are notoriously unsafe. It is surprising that they are being sold as safe contraceptives. Finally, there is the oldest safe commercial contraceptive on the market, the condom or rubber, as it is commonly called, which is used by the man. These are quite safe. But accidents result from careless use or a defect in the very thin latex rubber that they are made from.

Only you can decide for yourself whether you want to take the chances that are involved in finding the ultimate sexual satisfaction.

*One of the older sex courses - 1969 vintage

VII. A SOCIALIST SWEDISH AND COMMUNIST RUSSIAN MESSAGE

Los Angeles Times, March 1, 1964:

> "The sex education promoted by Sex Education Lobbies has existed in Sweden since 1954.
>
> The King's physician, Dr. Ulf Nordwall, and 140 eminent Swedish doctors and teachers signed a petition to their government expressing concern over sexual hysteria in the young. The petition asserted that this problem appeared to be a product of sex education, and it was now the business of the schools to correct it."

It may be of some interest to note that prior to the Russian Revolution, Russian Communists fanatically promoted sex education, free love, pornography and perversion. However, soon after the Communists gained control they quickly abolished these sexual practices. They seemed to know that no government could endure the destruction of marriage and family. These institutions were rapidly reestablished and virtually sanctified by the Soviet Union. Sex education was put to an end in 1924.

Why communists and thoughtlessly liberal groups in America insist that carnal sex education, free love, etc. are essential for our democratic society while at the same time they champion Russia's prohibiting such practices is perplexing.

VIII. MEDICS AND THE SEXUAL REVOLUTION

From earliest times Man has faithfully followed the advise of physicians.

Long ago, some medicine men decided that trephining (removing a circular section of bone from the skull) was the cure for medical ailments. This bizarre treatment was considered a primary "therapeutic" procedure despite the fact that trephining invariably worsened the patient's condition. In some cases, skulls found by archeologists show one, two, three and frequently more trephinings.

Pity the poor patient or medicine man who dared question the wisdom and the intended therapeutic results of medical leaders who recommended boring holes in people's heads. Like today, it would have taken a fearless, apolitical "surgeon general" to come forth with the conclusion: "Trephining may be injurious to your health."

After killing countless numbers of people, trephining gradually lost its popularity. It was replaced by another treatment that medical leaders, then, claimed was a sure cure for all ailments. Physicians throughout the world at that time were persuaded by their affluent leaders to rely on this new treatment — bloodletting. Sucking leeches were placed over a sick individual's body or knives were used to cut arteries to drain blood.

Bloodletting became the standard practice for treating malaria, tuberculosis, broken bones, hysteria, etc. It was prescribed for everything. Like trephining, bloodletting was responsible for the untimely deaths of countless humans (one of whom was President George Washington).

Nevertheless, for thousands of years, this practice was used by physicians blindly following the dictates of imperious medical authorities. Woe unto practicing physicians, such as Louis Pasteur, who spoke out disclaiming the rationality of treating patients with blood-sucking leeches. Only by the grace of providence did Pasteur manage to keep his head, much less his medical license.

Reluctantly, in the late nineteenth century, some world medical leaders conceded the errancy of bloodletting.

When bloodletting lost its status, physicians in the early twentieth century quickly replaced it with other irrational panaceas. Many doctors, it seems, have a propensity for quack nostrums.

Calomel — a whitish powder consisting of mercurous chloride — became a favorite medicine at the turn of the century. Medical leaders proclaimed that calomel should be used for treating a multitude of illnesses. The "scientific" rationale given to lemming physician followers was: "A little mercury poisoning won't kill you so it must be good for what ails you."

The calomel craze lasted from the late nineteenth century until the early 1940's. It was about this time that a new, young medical discipline was appearing on the scene — Psychiatry.

Not to be outdone by their trephining, bloodletting, calomel prescribing medical colleagues, psychiatrists of the late nineteenth and early twentienth century quickly made up their own fatuous panaceas for treating mental illnesses. By thoroughly misinterpreting the findings of Dr. Sigmund Freud, the 1900 psychiatrists proclaimed that anxiety states were due to a lack of sexual intercourse. Treatment, of course, consisted of having the patient engage in free-wheeling sex practices. Looking for affluent leadership to sanction their "new discoveries", they falsely attributed their new sex treatments to Freud himself.

Stunned by the serious harm that such innane psychiatric advice was causing, Freud felt compelled to forestall the self proclaimed sexperts. In 1910 he issued a warning in his article *WILD PSYCHOANALYSIS* (The Complete Works of Sigmund Freud—Vol. XI). In his paper Freud severely criticized psychiatrists who recommended free love as a cure for emotionally distressed patients.

Citing the case of one psychiatrist who had advised a woman patient to relieve her mental anxieties by engaging in sexual intercourse or masturbation, Freud said:

"I may do a man who is unknown to me (the physician) an injustice by connecting my remarks about Wild Psychoanalysis with this incident. But by so doing I may perhaps prevent others from doing harm to their patients....

The physician was ignorant of a number of scientific theories of psycho-analysis or had misapprehended them...The doctor's advice to the lady shows clearly in what sense he understands the expression 'sexual life' — namely, in which by sexual needs nothing is meant but the need for coitus or analgous acts producing orgasm and emission of the sexual substances....

The mental in sexual life should not be overlooked or underestimated. We use the word 'sexuality' in a comprehensive sense....We have long known that mental absence of satisfaction with all its consequences can exist where there is no lack of normal sexual intercourse.

Anyone not sharing this view of sexuality has no right to adduce psychoanalytic theses dealing with the importance of the sex act.

By emphasizing exclusively the physical factor in sexuality he (the physician) undoubtedly simplified the problem greatly....but he alone must bear the responsibility for what he does....

No one can ever believe that sexual satisfaction in itself constituted a remedy for the suffering of neurotics...."

Freud's admonitions were effective. Psychiatrists got the message, and psychiatry began making significant advancement up until the 1960's. Then, along came Calderone—SIECUS—Planned Parenthood. Freud was no longer around to temper them.

Freud's teachings were ignored. Free-love and perversions condoned by SIECUS and Planned Parenthood became fashionable. The modern psychiatrists and clinical psychologists began once again to worship the golden calf of physical sex. Sexual hedonistic practices were becoming the accepted creed for treating emotional problems. The current leaders had spoken.

In the early 1970's the American Psychiatric Association established "psychiatric bloodletting." The Association informed its members that henceforth perversions, such as homosexuality, were no longer to be considered mental illnesses. All perversions that were up until this time regarded as mental disorders were now to be considered as normal alternate life styles. SIECUS—Planned Parenthood eagerly supported the declaration of the American Psychiatric Association. (APA, SIECUS and PP paid no notice to the fact that the very foundation of psychoanalysis rested on the fact that sexual perversions were the ultimate mental illnesses.)

The proclamation of the American Psychiatric Association opened Pandora's Box. Latent homosexuals became blatantly overt. Many young people were converted into becoming homosexuals, and the homosexual population grew by leaps and bounds. Other perverts seemed to come out of the "woodwork." Carnal sex programs were confidently established in public schools everywhere.

Not only did psychiatrists, clinical psychologists and social workers climb aboard the SIECUS—Planned Parenthood—American Psychiatric Association bandwagon glorifying the golden calf of sexual hedonism, but physicians in other specialties readily joined in. The parade of uninhibited sex practices seemed to enthrall the latter day medicine men of the 20th century.

The public, as from earliest times, was prone to follow the dictates of the medical society. The culture of Western Civilization was depreciated. Sexual normalcy was out, base sexuality was in.

By means of illogical excuses, distorted statistics, and by disavowing clinical sexual truths, the SIECUS—Planned Parenthood—American Psychiatric Association hurled aside the objections of many conscientious, clinically experienced physicians who opposed them.

The highly cherished scientific approach, that was a part of the halcyon years of medicine lasting a few brief years between 1940-1960, was replaced by old "scientific" deceptions and quackery. Acupuncture, megavitamins, meaningless formulas and theories and above all, pagan sex practices became many modern physicians' armamentarium.

If it weren't for medicines, such as penicillin and other life saving pharmaceutical products, and if it were not for the advanced mechanical breakthroughs provided by the manufacturers of technical medical equipment, many of today's medicine men would be at the same scientific level as his brethren of ancient times.

Freudian psychoanalysts provide an oasis of truth for civilized sexual needs. But these sources have kept a low profile. They seem determined to avoid confrontation with and possible ostracism by the powerful SIECUS, Planned Parenthood and the American Psychiatric Association triumverate.

Come back Moses. Come back Freud. Physicians are once again worshipping the golden calf of sexual degeneracy, destroying themselves and their followers.

IX. A CASE IN POINT:
THE HINDMARSH MURDERS

An egregious example of the uncontrolled, savage sexual behavior in an adolescent living in an affluent community can be seen in a news article appearing in the June 15, 1985 *Los Angeles Times*:

"CRYBABY", 17*, GETS 69 YEARS TO LIFE
IN TWO SEX SLAYINGS

By Tim Waters, Times Staff Writer

....A judge on Friday sentenced a Rancho Palos Verdes teenager to 69 years to life in prison on convictions of sexually molesting and murdering two young girls.

Superior court Judge Cecil Mills imposed the sentence on Kevin Earl Hindmarsh, who was found guilty last February on *two counts each of murder and sodomy with a foreign object* in the slayings of the 11-year-old Palos Verdes Peninsula girls.

....after listening to a tearful plea by one of the victim's mothers, that Hindmarsh should be sent to prison, Mills handed down the maximum sentence allowed under law.

Based on his reading of a psychological report, the judge said he believed Hindmarsh is "sociopathic"....

The victims, Neda O'Sullivan and her friend, Kristin Joy Macknight, were found beaten and sexually assaulted in a condominium in the gated Palos Verdes complex where Neda lived with her mother....Neda was already dead. Kristin died the next day at a hospital.

Defense attorney Fredricks has said that he will appeal the conviction.

*Earl Hindmarsh was probably 14 or 15 when he committed these murders.

The following interpretations are entirely hypothetical. No claim is made as to their accuracy; they are highly speculative. My aim is only to suggest some explanation for the Hindmarsh murders.

172

The area in which Neda O'Sullivan and Kristin Macknight were found murdered was gated. No evidence of forced entry was reported in the *Los Angeles Times* news article. Possibly Hindmarsh joined the girls in the condominium at their invitation.

Eleven-year-old girls have no desire for the sex act. However, they have a normal sexual curiosity. Neda lived in a California community that was among the first to establish sex education in its schools. It is logical to infer that she and Kristin attended sex classes which interfered with the normal development of their sexual curiosity.

Sexual curiosity in preteen girls is naturally satisfied in private discussions between two girlfriends sharing a close companionship. The individualistic opinions expressed are a part of preteen sensuality and are an early step towards developing independence. Direct sexual information provided preteenagers by sex instructors disrupt this stage of sexual growth.

Due to school sex teachings, Neda and Kristin may have been tempted to act out their sexual curiosity with Hindmarsh instead of sharing "sexual secrets" with each other. Hindmarsh may have become involved in this way.

The school sex programs to which Hindmarsh may have been subjected during his latency years could easily have retarded compassionate feelings and pity for others. Additionally, he may have been taught that sodomy and other perversities were simply normal variations.

Sodomy and sadism seemed to appeal to Hindmarsh more than sexual intercourse. Tim Waters in his news report makes no mention of the girls having been involved in genital sex.

Sex educators regarding sodomy as normal, should inform their students that sodomous acts can cause serious infections, hemorrhoids, anal fissures and perforation of the intestinal wall followed by irreversible peritonitis. (The anus is most heavily filled with pathogenic bacteria. Puncturing the anus and allowing these infectious agents to enter the abdominal cavity is always a life threatening situation.)

Though it is difficult to feel sympathy for Hindmarsh, perhaps, he should be pitied. He must have had a vestige of compassion in his soul as evidenced by his crying in court, which earned him the name "Crybaby." His crying is an indication he felt some pity - at least for himself.

As previously mentioned, SIECUS—Planned Parenthood sex education would have students believe (1) that girls relieved of false sexual inhibitions feel unbridled passion for sex, (2) that values and standards depend on enjoying what you do and doing what you enjoy (3) "Sex is for fun."

One can visualize Kevin Earl Hindmarsh seated on his prison cot, thighs up against his chest, chin resting in the palms of his hands while he gazes at the cell wall and ponders: "I meant no harm. I beat them only because they had hang-ups and wouldn't have fun with me. What did I do wrong? Why am I being punished?"

He was simply doing what he had been taught.

Hindmarsh, I believe, is too far gone to be allowed in everday society. But what about carnal sex education and the pornographic media? In my opinion, they are probably the primary causes destroying the lives of Hindmarsh and two eleven-year-old girls and for causing interminable grief for the parents of these three young people.